FINDING-OUT BOOKS

WHY THINGS CHANGE

The Story of Evolution

Written by Jeanne Bendick

Illustrated by Karen Bendick Watson

Parents' Magazine Press—New York

Library of Congress Cataloging in Publication Data

Bendick, Jeanne.
    Why things change.

    (Finding-out books)
    SUMMARY: Describes simply the process of evolution
and how it resulted in the plants and animals of the
world today.
    1. Evolution—Juvenile literature.   [1. Evolution]
I. Watson, Karen Bendick, 1948—   illus.
II. Title.
QH367.1.B45   575   72-13430
ISBN 0-8193-0682-7

CONTENTS

Introduction   4

What Is Evolution?   10

How Slow Is Slow?   12

What Makes Things Change?   14

One Kind of Change Makes Another   16

Rules for Surviving   18

The First and Biggest Difference   26

The Plants Come Ashore   42

The Animals Move Ashore   44

Here Come the Reptiles   46

Now, A Different Kind of Animal   50

People Are Different   58

Faster and Faster   60

Index   63

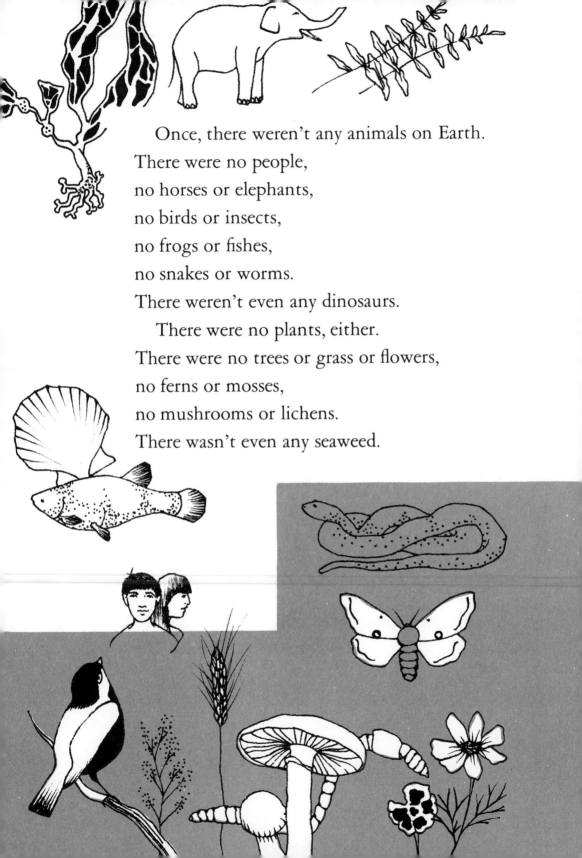

Once, there weren't any animals on Earth.
There were no people,
no horses or elephants,
no birds or insects,
no frogs or fishes,
no snakes or worms.
There weren't even any dinosaurs.
  There were no plants, either.
There were no trees or grass or flowers,
no ferns or mosses,
no mushrooms or lichens.
There wasn't even any seaweed.

There were no living things at all.

About 5 billion years ago, when planet Earth was new, there were only fire, earthquakes and volcanoes, hot melting rock, steam and water, rising and raining, rising and raining.

It took a couple of billion years for Earth to just cool and settle down. But still there were no living things.

There was some land. And there was lots of water. But the land was only rock. There was no soil.

And the water was only water with a lot of chemicals in it that had been washed out of the steaming, cooling Earth over 2 billion years.

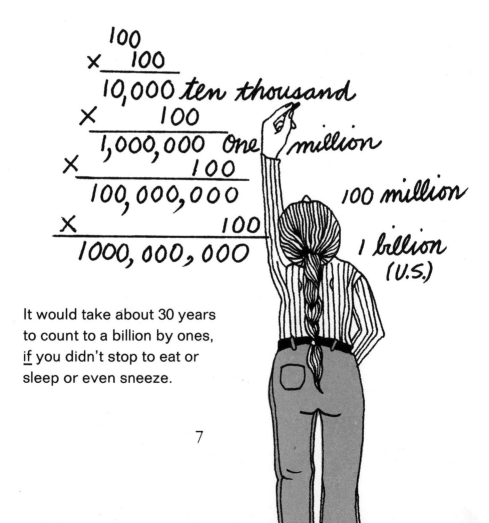

$$
\begin{array}{r}
100 \\
\times \quad 100 \\
\hline
10,000 \text{ ten thousand} \\
\times \quad 100 \\
\hline
1,000,000 \text{ One million} \\
\times \quad 100 \\
\hline
100,000,000 \quad 100 \text{ million} \\
\times \quad 100 \\
\hline
1000,000,000 \quad 1 \text{ billion (U.S.)}
\end{array}
$$

It would take about 30 years to count to a billion by ones, <u>if</u> you didn't stop to eat or sleep or even sneeze.

7

Then somehow—nobody is exactly sure how—over a long, long time some of the chemicals in those first warm oceans came together in a very special way into tiny specks of living stuff.

They were not plants.

They were not animals.

They were much too small to see. But they were alive.

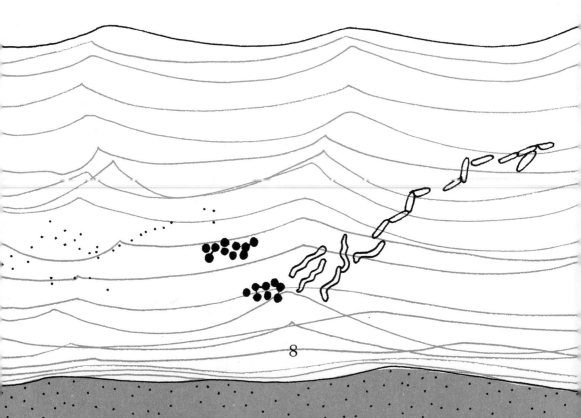

And over the next 3 billion years or so, those
much-too-small-to-see living specks
changed
and changed
and changed
into all the kinds of living things on Earth today,
living in all the different places.

The word for how all that happened is *evolution.*

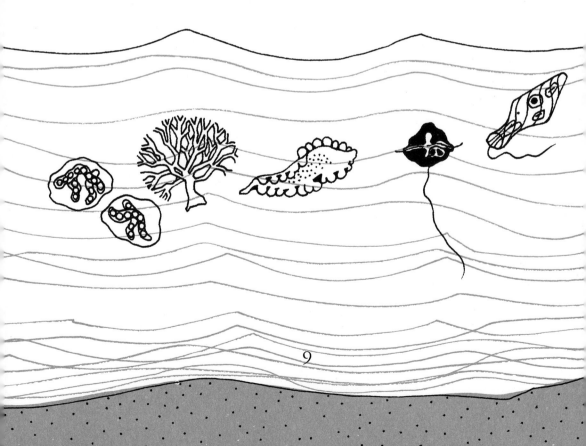

WHAT IS EVOLUTION?

Evolution is one thing changing, or evolving, into another. But not fast. And only in a special kind of way.

You can't say that spring evolves into summer, or that water evolves into ice, or that clouds evolve into rain, even if those things do change, one into another. Just changing isn't evolution.

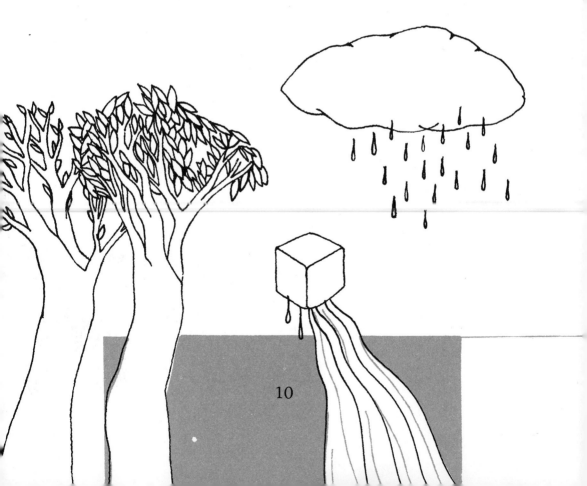

10

You couldn't even say that an acorn evolves into an oak tree, or that a caterpillar evolves into a butterfly. Growing up isn't evolution.

When people talk about evolution they usually mean the slow changing of living things so they can keep on going in the changing world around them.

HOW SLOW IS SLOW?

It's hard to even think about how slowly living things evolve. It's hard to think about how much time it has taken, up to now.

Making a kind of picture of all that time and what happened in it should help.

Take a roll of shelf paper and mark off 5 feet on it. Leave an extra foot or so on top, then cut the paper off and tape it up.

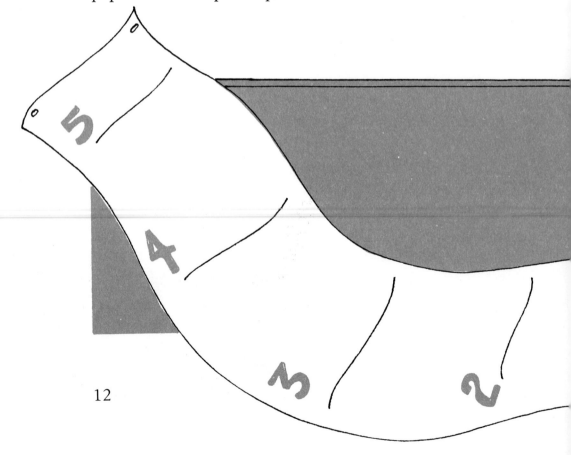

12

Make a line at the bottom, where you began measuring, and number the line 0. That's about when Earth began, on your time chart.

Make a line at each one foot mark and number the lines 1, 2, 3, 4, 5. The space between each line stands for one billion years.

Between 0 and 2 is the time it took for Earth to cool down—2 billion years. For all that time there was nothing alive. And then there were those living, slowly changing specks.

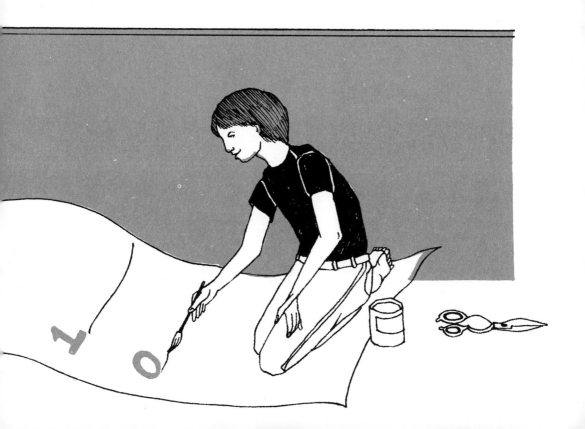

WHAT MAKES THINGS CHANGE?

Everything on Earth changes and keeps on changing.

The shape of Earth changes. Wind and weather wear away mountains. Land washes into the sea. New land rises out of the sea. New mountains rise out of the land. Even the continents move away from each other over a long, long time.

14

As Earth changes in different places, the climate changes. It gets hot. It gets cold. Sometimes it's wet for a long time. Then it's dry for a long time.

And as the climate changes, living things change. Old kinds of plants die and different kinds of plants evolve.

Old kinds of animals change and evolve into different kinds of animals.

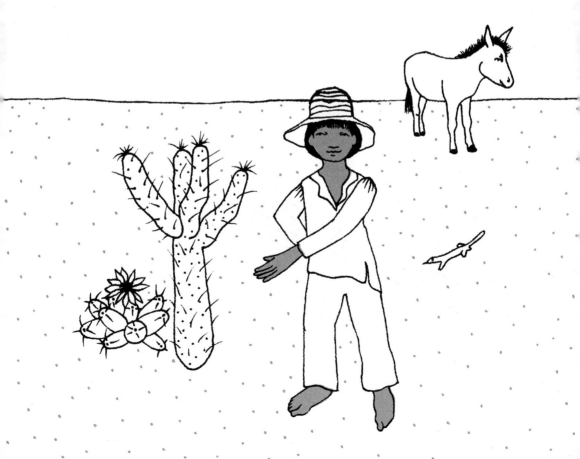

ONE KIND OF CHANGE MAKES ANOTHER

Nothing just changes by itself. All changes are connected.

When the climate is wet for a long time, plants evolve that use a lot of water.

If the climate gets dry, the only plants that can stay alive are those that can get along without much water.

When the climate changes, the plants that can't change too die out. They can't *survive*.

When plants change, animals change, because all animals depend on plants for food. Some animals eat plants. The animals that don't eat plants eat the animals that eat plants.

So if the climate changes, and the kinds of plants change, the kinds of animals that live in that place have to change too. If they can't, they can't survive. They die out.

Every living thing has its place in the food chain.

MILK

CACTI LIVE IN
THE DESERT

RULES FOR SURVIVING

When we talk about plants and animals surviving we don't usually mean one particular plant or one particular animal. We mean all the plants and animals in a group.

For a kind of plant or animal to survive it must be a success.

18

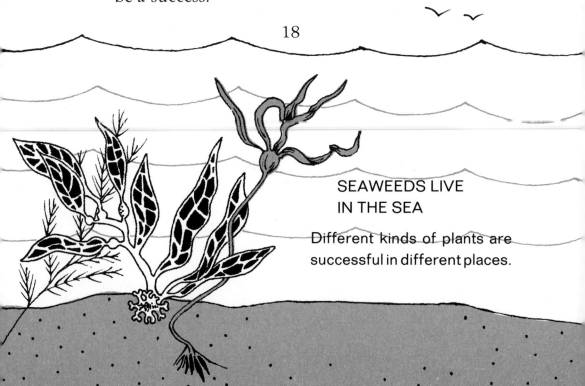

SEAWEEDS LIVE
IN THE SEA

Different kinds of plants are successful in different places.

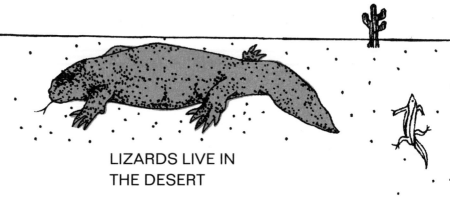

LIZARDS LIVE IN
THE DESERT

A successful plant or animal doesn't mean that it is famous. It means that it is fitted, or *adapted,* to the life it lives. Everything about it is just right for living in a special place, getting the food it needs, escaping from its enemies.

A successful kind of plant or animal also has to make enough other living things like itself so that its kind of living thing keeps on going.

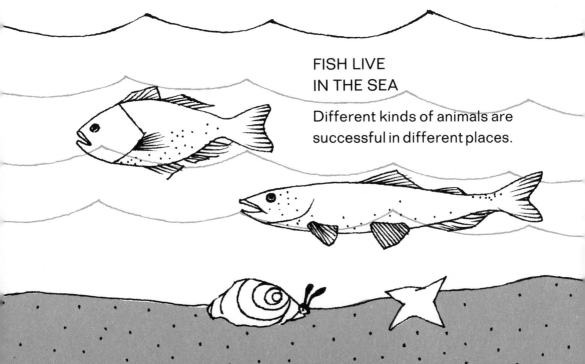

FISH LIVE
IN THE SEA

Different kinds of animals are successful in different places.

But there is one more rule for surviving. Some of those new living things must be different—a little different or a lot—from their parents.

Maybe the different ones are not quite as well adapted as their parents to the world they all live in. But maybe some of them are fitted *better* than their parents to live in a world that's about to change in some way.

As horses evolved, do you think that being bigger made them more successful?

Then, about the size of a donkey

About 50 million years ago, the size of a fox

Then, about the size of a big dog

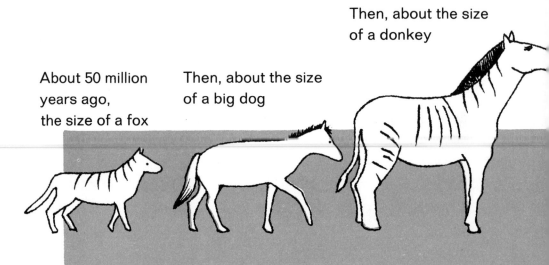

When things change, even the most successful plants and animals can't adapt overnight to survive. So the survival of a kind of plant or animal often depends on the different ones that happen to be better fitted to the new conditions in the world around them.

Horses like the ones we know have been around for about a million years.

Ever since the first living specks appeared on Earth, that's the kind of thing that happened. Every time something in the world changed, the living things that could get along best with those changes survived.

Maybe they hadn't been successful up to then. Maybe they were just about getting on and other plants or animals were the successful, important ones.

Then, when something changed, some of those different ones became the successful ones and the plants and animals that weren't adapted to the changes didn't make it. They became *extinct*.

Once a kind of plant or animal becomes extinct, that's the end of them. They can never start up again.

23

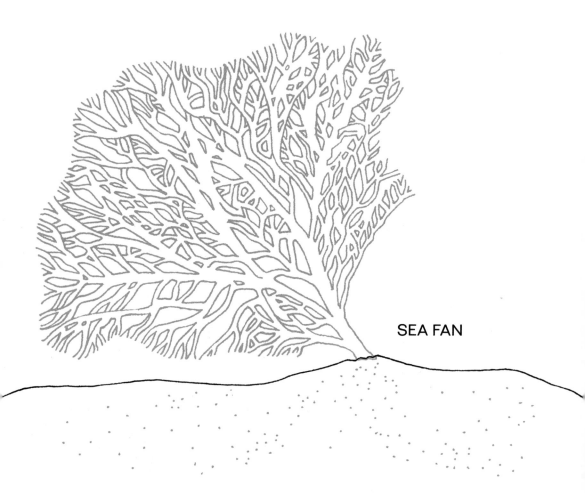

SEA FAN

But evolution doesn't mean that *only* the plants and animals that change can survive.

Some kinds of living things can survive just the way they are through all the kinds of changes that go on around them. That's because they are not too special. They can live successfully under many different conditions.

Some kinds of living things have been around for billions of years and they are still doing fine.

All these are animals.

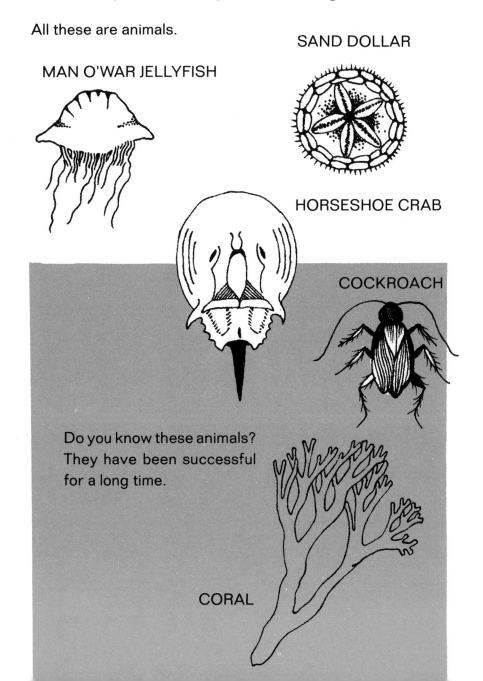

MAN O'WAR JELLYFISH

SAND DOLLAR

HORSESHOE CRAB

COCKROACH

Do you know these animals? They have been successful for a long time.

CORAL

THE FIRST AND BIGGEST
DIFFERENCE

Those first specks of life, drifting in the warm
seas, needed what all living things need to stay alive
and to keep living things going.

They needed food, oxygen, water, and a way to
make new living things like themselves.

The water and oxygen were all around them. For
"food" they took in chemicals from the water.
When they got bigger, they split apart. One speck
became two specks.

Over a long, long time, some of them became different—nobody knows how. The different ones became adapted to use sunlight to make their own food inside themselves, for themselves.

These were the beginnings of plants. Only plants can use light to make food. Of all the differences that came after, this was the most important for living things.

Other specks never became adapted to make their own food. They had to get it some other way.

Some became adapted to eat the food makers.

Some became adapted to eat each other.

No animals can make their own food. They have to get it by eating plants, or by eating other animals that eat plants.

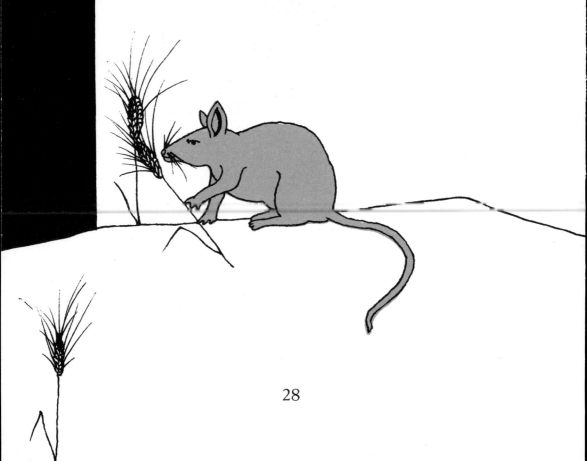

So, to survive, most animals have to move around. They have to move to where the plants are. Or they have to move to catch other animals.

Over a long, long time, animals evolved different ways of moving to catch the different things they ate.

Different animals are adapted to get their food in different ways.

At first all those beginning plants and animals were very simple. They had one cell. That one cell could do everything it needed to do for its kind of living thing to survive.

There are still one-celled plants and animals. If you have a chance to look through a microscope you can probably see some of them in any drop of water from a pond, a river, or the ocean.

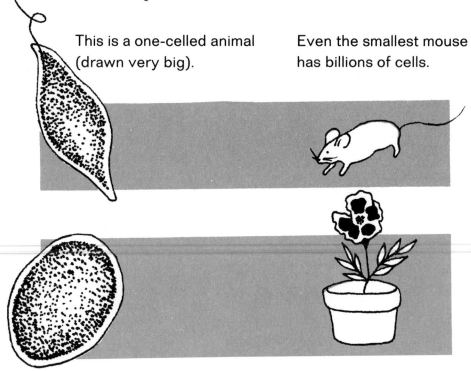

This is a one-celled animal (drawn very big).

Even the smallest mouse has billions of cells.

This is a one-celled plant (drawn very big).

Even a flower in a flowerpot has billions of cells.

How long did it take for those first living specks to evolve into one-celled plants and animals? It doesn't seem like much to happen.

Draw a line on your chart, halfway between the 2 and the 3. If you want to, draw some of these one-celled plants and animals there. Below them, make some specks down to the 2.

It took about half a billion years for the specks to evolve into one-celled plants and animals.

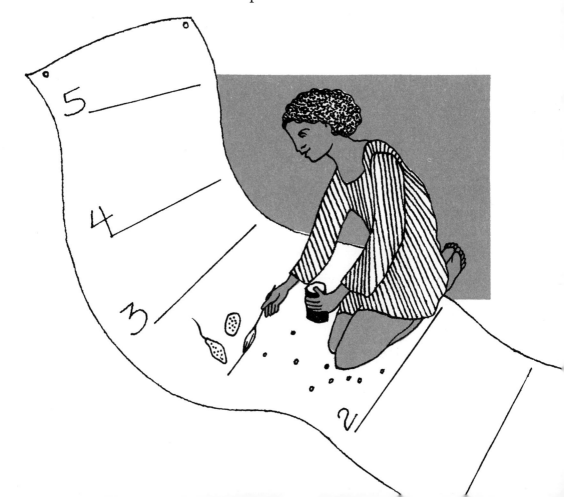

Plants and animals kept on changing. Some cells joined together to make bigger, more complex plants and animals. Over a long, long time some added parts and some lost parts they weren't using any more.

But why didn't all the plants evolve into the same kind of plants? How did there come to be pine trees and pear trees, seaweeds and milkweeds, potatoes and rice?

Why didn't all the animals evolve into the same kind of animals? How did there come to be eels and elephants, owls and turtles, beetles and people?

Because the world kept changing. In different places it changed in different ways.

In some places the changes were big—as big as new mountains or deserts, fresh water rivers, continents drifting apart and oceans flowing into new places.

In some places the changes were small—as small as a new kind of plant starting to grow, or a small animal moving in that had never lived there before.

And in each of those different places, the living things evolved in different ways to survive in their own place. So all around Earth plants got more different from each other. And so did animals.

There are many more different kinds of animals than there are plants. There are more than a million kinds of animals and about one-quarter million kinds of plants.

One reason for that is that animals had to evolve all kinds of different ways of getting or catching the food that was around.

They had to adapt to eat different kinds of food so there would be enough for them all.

They had to adapt to live in all the places where plants grow.

Some of them had to adapt to escape from the animals that ate them.

Insects are animals. So are birds and fish, reptiles and amphibians, mollusks, spiders, and more.

36

If plants have sunlight, air, water, and growing space they can make their own food.

They can't escape from enemies. They just keep growing and making new plants. So plants are not as different from each other as animals are.

Trees are plants. So are grass and bushes, ferns, vegetables, and more.

About half a billion years ago there were still no animals on land but the sea was full of life. There were jellyfish, sponges and starfish, sea urchins and sand dollars, snails, clams, and worms.

The most important animals were the trilobites. They were something like shrimp and they came in all sizes. The trilobites were the most important animals for 300 million years, but they are extinct now.

Most of those other sea animals are still around.

39

Meantime, another kind of animal was evolving on the muddy bottoms of freshwater streams. It didn't look like much but it had something new. It had brains.

Over the next 75 million years some of them changed until they were a lot like some of the fishes that are still around. They got backbones and skeletons, fins, teeth, and tails. They got bigger and faster. Their brains and senses got better.

About 400 million years ago, and then for another 50 million years, the fishes were the most important animals. Can you find the place to put them on the chart?

THE PLANTS COME ASHORE

And the world kept changing. The seas became shallow along the shore and some of the sea plants were different enough to be able to live on the rocks at the edge of the sea. They were just some flat, gray-green stuff on the rocks. Plants like that are still around.

Those first land plants changed and grew until there were plants like the ones on this page and they are still around.

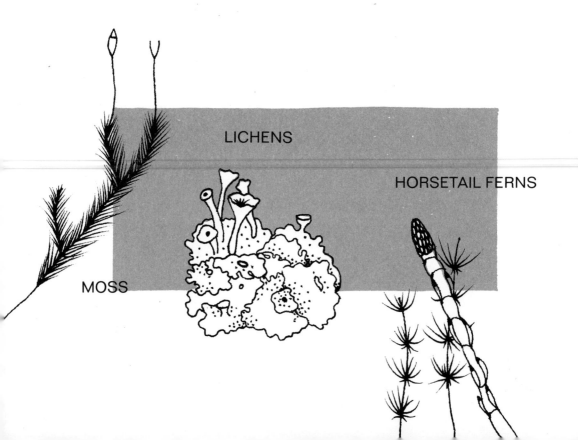

LICHENS

HORSETAIL FERNS

MOSS

And then there were great forests of ferns
growing farther and farther across the land.

As the land plants died and fell, they made soil,
deeper and deeper. When there was soil to hold
their roots and to grow in, bigger plants could
evolve. So now there could be trees. Not yet, but
they were coming.

There were still no animals on land. But when
plants came ashore, it was possible for animals to
live there, too. Animals live where the food is.

THE ANIMALS MOVE ASHORE

There was one group of fishes that was sort of a freak. It had stumpy little fins instead of flat, streamlined ones, so it wasn't much of a swimmer. It had evolved lungs for breathing air, while other fish got their oxygen much more easily from the water. The new group wasn't very successful.

But the world was still changing. The shallow seas began drying up, leaving ponds and puddles without much oxygen in them. In those places, the water breathers couldn't survive. But the new group, gulping the air it needed, managed. It could even drag itself from pond to pond on its stumpy fins.

The first air-breathing animal looked something like this.

It wasn't a real land animal yet. It laid its eggs in the water and they hatched there. It was the beginning of the amphibians—animals that spend part of their life in the water and part on land. Some amphibians are still around—the frogs, toads, and salamanders.

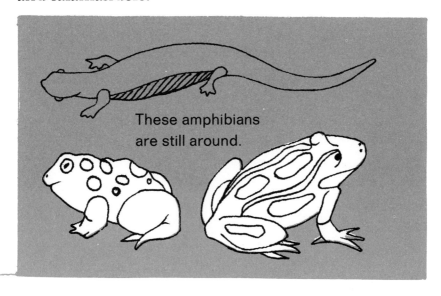

These amphibians are still around.

At about the same time, other land animals were evolving from the last of the trilobites. They were the scorpions, the spiders, and the first insects.

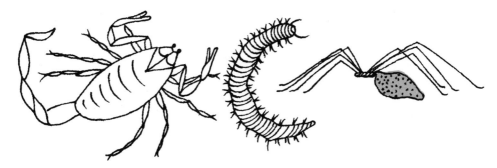

HERE COME THE REPTILES

The amphibians themselves were never really important animals. But they were important as a bridge between sea animals and land animals. The next really important animals, the reptiles, evolved out of the amphibians.

Reptiles were real land animals. They laid their eggs on land and they could live there. They were so well fitted to life in the warm and steamy fern forests and swamps that after a while Earth was full of them.

The biggest land animals that ever lived—the dinosaurs—were reptiles. The dinosaurs were so well adapted that 180 million years ago, and for 150 million years after that, they were the most important animals. Then the climate changed so much that the dinosaurs weren't adapted any more and they didn't survive.

But the dinosaurs weren't the only reptiles.
There were small dinosaur relatives, the lizards.

There were legless reptiles, the snakes.

There were reptiles with shells, the turtles.

There were reptiles that lived in the water,
like the crocodiles.

Those reptiles are still around.

There were flying reptiles too. They are extinct, but one kind was the ancestor of all the birds on Earth.

NOW, A DIFFERENT KIND OF ANIMAL

For 100 million years, another kind of animal had been evolving from the reptiles. They didn't look important. They looked something like small, furry lizards. Instead of shells or scales, they had hair all over.

They were warm-blooded. The temperature of their blood stayed the same no matter how hot or cold the air around them was.

Fishes, amphibians, reptiles, and insects are cold-blooded. Their blood temperature changes. If it gets very cold around them, their blood gets so cold they can hardly move. If it gets very hot, so does their blood.

These new animals didn't lay eggs. The mothers carried the young inside themselves until they were ready to be born.

They had good brains, good senses, and they were fast on their feet.

These so-far unimportant little animals were the first mammals. They certainly were different from all the animals before them. But were they successful?

For a hundred million years, all the special things about mammals didn't matter much. The climate was warm, so fur and warm blood weren't very useful. And unprotected eggs did just as well as the young animals that were carried in their mothers' warm insides.

There was plenty of food around, so good brains and good senses weren't all that important either, even though the mammals needed a lot more food than other animals. (It takes much more energy to be a warm-blooded animal than a cold-blooded one.)

The mammals needed so much energy that they might not have made it if a new kind of plant had not spread around Earth. These were plants with flowers that made seeds. The seeds popped and blew and flew all over Earth so that there were seeds and grasses to eat, and fruit and roots and leaves and all the kinds of food that come from flowering plants.

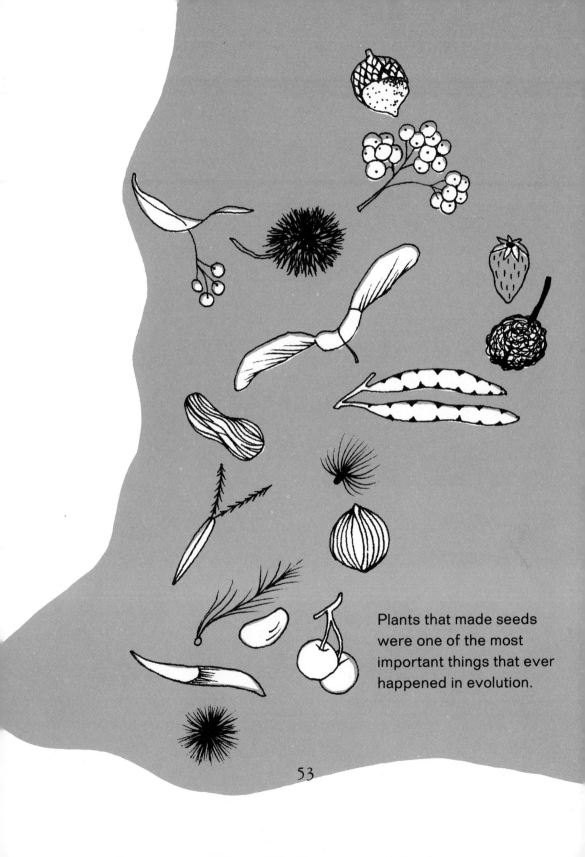

Plants that made seeds
were one of the most
important things that ever
happened in evolution.

53

And then, in many places, big mountains began to push up through the continents and the weather changed. It got drier and colder and the dinosaurs weren't adapted any more.

But the mammals were perfectly adapted to this kind of weather. They became the most important animals on Earth.

That was about 100 million years ago. Make a line on your chart about an inch below the 5. Between then and now, all the kinds of mammals that are still around evolved.

There are flying mammals, like bats,
and mammals that live in the water, like whales and
porpoises.
There are plant eaters with hoofs, like cows and
horses,
and plant gnawers with paws, like beavers and
rabbits.
There are meat eaters with paws and claws, like
bears and tigers,
and the primates, like monkeys.

Out of one of the primates (nobody is really sure which one!) came the next important animal. Draw a line about ¼ inch down from the 5.

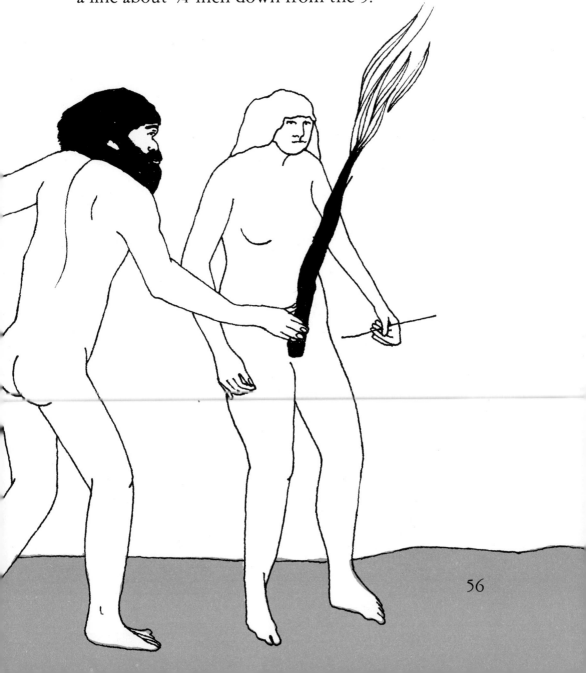

Above that are the mammals called humans.

There aren't many differences between early people and people now.

PEOPLE ARE DIFFERENT

People are a new kind of animal on Earth. Because the special thing about them is their wonderful brain, they can think and they can plan. They can learn and imagine and look ahead. They don't have to adapt to the changing Earth to survive. They can change the world around them instead.

They can make the places they live hotter or colder. They build shelter where they want it. They can move water from one place to another and move food to where they are, instead of spending their lives looking for it.

With tools and machines they can do anything any animal before them ever did. If they want to, they can even live in the air or under the sea.

As far as anyone knows now, people have only been around about 2 ½ million years. That's not very long, as evolution goes. And they have only been the most important animal for about 35,000 years—hardly a tick of the time clock. Do you think they will always be the most important animal?

FASTER AND FASTER

If you look at your evolution picture now, you can see some interesting things.

You can see that no kind of plant or animal just started up out of nowhere. Each kind evolved from a plant or animal that lived before it.

You can see that evolution never repeats itself. There's always something new. And newer usually means better. (Scientists say "higher.")

You can see that evolution seems to go faster and faster. Do you think that that's because the more kinds of living things there are, the more chances there are for new kinds to evolve?

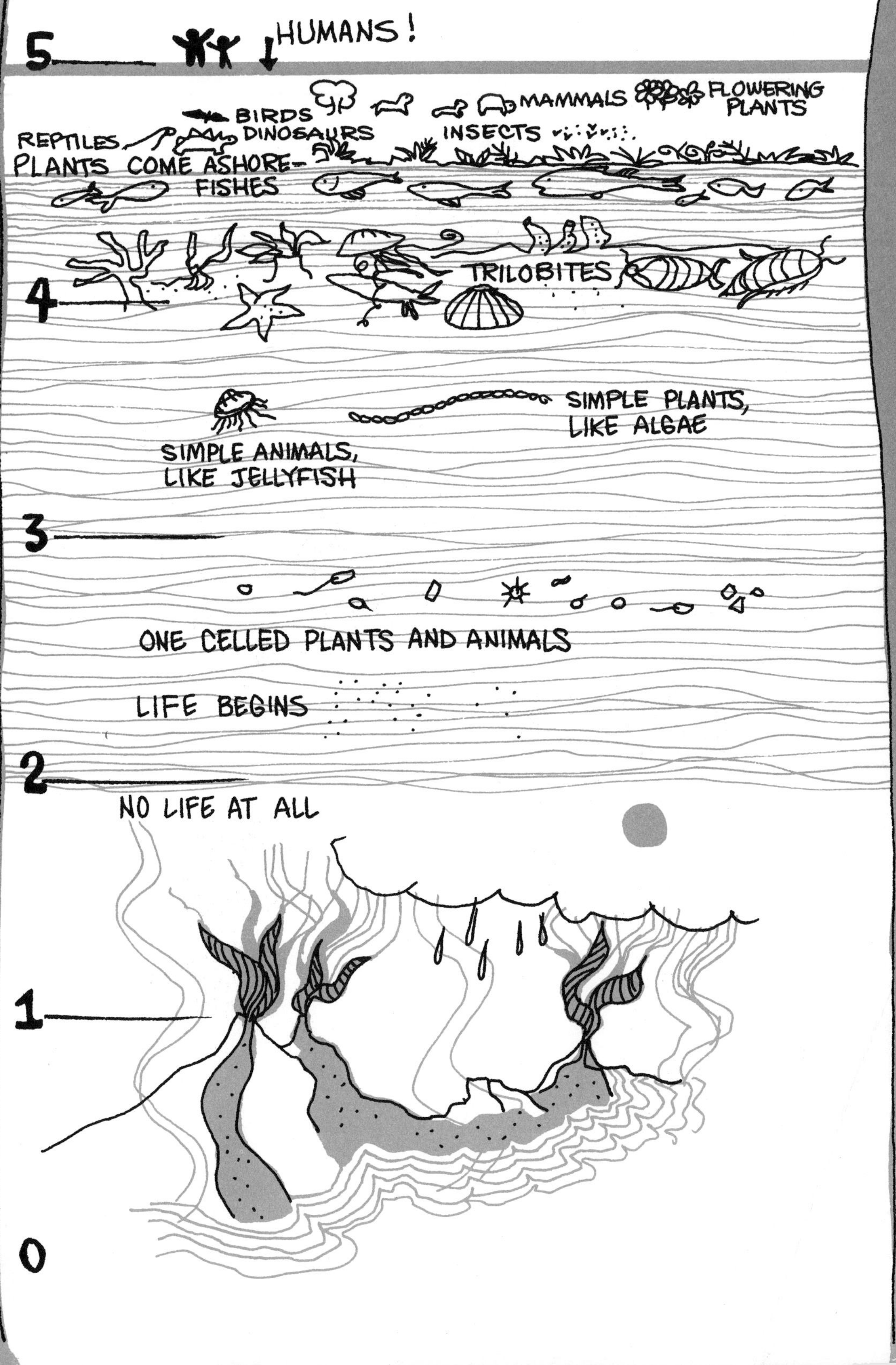

5 — HUMANS!

FLOWERING PLANTS

MAMMALS

BIRDS

DINOSAURS

INSECTS

REPTILES

PLANTS COME ASHORE—

FISHES

TRILOBITES

4 —

SIMPLE PLANTS, LIKE ALGAE

SIMPLE ANIMALS, LIKE JELLYFISH

3 —

ONE CELLED PLANTS AND ANIMALS

LIFE BEGINS

2 —

NO LIFE AT ALL

1 —

0

Do you think that evolution is over? Or do you think it's still going on?

Have you any ideas about what living things might be like in the future? If you have, draw them on your chart, above the 5.

INDEX

adaptation, 19-21, 22, 27;
  and food, 28;
  and motion, 29;
  animals and, 36;
  of mammals, 54
amphibians, 37, 45, 46, 50
animals, 8, 37;
  evolution of, 15;
  plants and, 17;
  survival of, 17, 18-21;
  successful, 18-19, 21, 22;
  becoming extinct, 22;
  and food, 28-29, 36, 43;
  moving of, 29, 34;
  one-celled, 30-31;
  changing of, 33;
  different kinds of, 34, 36;
  and adaptation, 36;
  and land, 38, 43, 44, 45, 46, 47;
  and sea, 38-39, 46;
  part-water, part-land, 45;
  warm-blooded, 50;
  cold-blooded, 50

bats, 55
bears, 55
beavers, 55
beetles, 33
birds, 4, 36, 49
brains, 51, 52;
  first animals with, 40-41;
  people and, 58
bushes, 37

cacti, 18
cells, of plants and animals, 30-32
changes, 9, 22, 27;
  and evolution, 10-11;
  on Earth, 14-15;
  connections between, 16;
  living things and, 22;
  big and small, 34;
  see also evolution
chemicals, 8, 26
clams, 38
climate, changes in, 15, 47;
  plants and, 16, 17;
  animals and, 17, 47
continents, 14, 34
cows, 55
crocodiles, 48

deserts, 18, 19, 34
dinosaurs, 4, 47, 48

Earth, before living things, 4-7, 13;
  cooling of, 6, 7, 13;
  first living things on, 8-9, 13, 22;
  time-chart for, 12-13, see also time-chart;
  shape of, 14;
  changes on, 14-15
earthquakes, 6
eels, 33
eggs, 45, 46
elephants, 4, 33
enemies, of plants and animals, 36, 37
evolution, 9, 34;
  definition of, 10-11;
  of plants and animals, 15, 32, 33;
  survival and, 24, 25;
  in streams, 40;
  from trilobites, 45;
  of mammals, 54;
  interesting things about, 60-61;
  and future, 62;
  see also change
extinct, meaning of, 22

ferns, 4, 37, 42, 43
fire, 6
fish, 4, 19, 36, 41, 44, 50
flowers, 4, 30
food, need of, 26;
  making of, 27, 28;
  and adaptation, 28;
  animals and, 28-29, 36, 43, 53;
  plants and, 37
food chain, 17
frogs, 4, 45

grass, 4, 37
growing up, and evolution, 11

horses, 4, 20, 21, 55
humans, see people

insects, 4, 36, 45, 50

jellyfish, 38

land, 7, 14
land animals, see under animals
lichens, 4, 42

living things, and Earth, 4-7, 9;
   first, 8-9, 22;
   slowness of evolution of, 11-13;
   changing of, 15;
   reproduction of, 19, 26;
   differences in, 20-21;
   needs of, 26;
   evolution and survival of, 34;
   and future, 62
lizards, 19, 48

mammals, 51-56
milkweeds, 32
mollusks, 36
monkeys, 55
mosses, 4, 42
mountains, 14, 34, 54
mouse, cells of, 30
moving, animals and, 29
mushrooms, 4

oceans, 8, 34;
owls, 33
oxygen, need of, 26

pear trees, 32
people, 4, 33, 58-59;
   evolution of, 56
pine trees, 32
plants, 4, 8, 36;
   evolution of, 15;
   climate and, 16;
   survival of, 16, 18-21;
   animals and, 17;
   successful, 18-19, 21, 22;
   becoming extinct, 22;
   beginning of, 27;
   one-celled, 30-31;
   changing of, 32;
   new, 34, 37;
   different kinds of, 34, 37;
   and enemies, 37;
   and food, 37;
   sea, changes in, 42;
   first land, 42-43;
   making of soil by, 43
porpoises, 55
potatoes, 32
primates, 55, 56

rabbits, 55
rain, 6

reproduction, 19, 26, 51, 52
reptiles, 36, 46-50;
   flying, 49;
   evolution from, 50
rice, 32
rivers, 34
rock, 6, 7

salamanders, 45
sand dollars, 38
scorpions, 45
sea, land and, 14;
   seaweeds and, 18;
   fish and, 19;
   changes in, 42, 44
sea animals, *see under* animals
sea urchins, 38
seaweed, 4, 18, 32
seeds, from plants, 52, 53
snails, 38
snakes, 4, 48
soil, 7, 43
spiders, 36, 45
sponges, 38
starfish, 38
success, 18-19, 21, 22, 24, 25
sunlight, and food, 27
survival, 16-21, 22, 24, 25, 34, 44

tigers, 55
time-chart, 12-13, 60-61;
   and one-celled plants and animals, 31;
   fish and, 41;
   and mammals, 54;
   humans and, 56;
   and future, 62
toads, 45
trees, 4, 37, 43
trilobites, 39, 45
turtles, 13, 48

vegetables, 37
volcanoes, 6

water, 6, 7;
   plants and, 16;
   need of, 26;
   breathers of, 44
weather, 14, 54
whales, 55
wind, and mountains, 14
world, changes in, 34, 42, 44
worms, 4, 38